THE ULTIMATE

10

Entertainment

AMUSEMENT PARK RIDES

WITHDRAWN

By Susan K. Mitchell

Gareth Stevens
Publishing

Please visit our web site at **www.garethstevens.com**.
For a free catalog describing Gareth Stevens Publishing's list of high-quality books, call 1-800-542-2595 (USA) or 1-800-387-3178 (Canada). Gareth Stevens Publishing's fax: 1-877-542-2596

Library of Congress Cataloging-in-Publication Data
Mitchell, Susan K.
    Amusement park rides / by Susan K. Mitchell.
      p. cm. — (The ultimate 10. Entertainment)
    Includes bibliographical references and index.
    ISBN-10: 0-8368-9162-7   ISBN-13: 978-0-8368-9162-1 (lib. bdg.)
    ISBN-10: 1-4339-2210-X   ISBN-13: 978-1-4339-2210-7 (pbk.)
    1. Amusement rides—Juvenile literature. I. Title.
  GV1859.M58 2009
  791.06'8—dc22   2009008291

This edition first published in 2010 by
Gareth Stevens Publishing
A Weekly Reader® Company
1 Reader's Digest Road
Pleasantville, NY 10570-7000 USA

Executive Managing Editor: Lisa M. Herrington
Senior Designer: Keith Plechaty

Produced by Editorial Directions, Inc.

Art Direction and Page Production: The Design Lab

Picture credits
Key: t = top, b = bottom
Cover, title page: (t) Shutterstock, (c) Russell Simmons, (b) Shutterstock; pp. 4-5: Images courtesy of Dreamworld@Gold Coast, Australia; p. 6:Shutterstock; p. 7: Stan Honda/AFP/Getty Images; p. 8: © Noah K. Murray/Star Ledger/Corbis; p. 9: (t) AP Photo/Mike Dere, (b) Shutterstock; p. 10: Shutterstock; p. 11: Coasterimage.com; p. 12: (t) Coasterimage.com, (b) AP Photo/Paul M. Walsh; p. 13: (t) William Manning/Corbis, (b) Shutterstock; p. 14: Shutterstock; p. 15: Joel A. Rogers; p. 16: Toru Yamanaka/AFP/Getty Images; p. 17: (t) ©Michael S. Yamashita/Corbis, (b) Shutterstock; p. 18: Shutterstock; p. 19: AP Photo/Al Behrman, File; p. 20: AP Photo/Rick Norton; p. 21: (t) AP Photo/Al Behrman, (b) Shutterstock; p. 22: Shutterstock; p. 23: Coasterimage.com; p. 24: Coaster Grotto; p. 25: (t) Coaster Grotto; p. 26: Shutterstock; p. 27: Mathew Imaging/WireImage; p. 28: Coaster Grotto; p. 29: (t) Coaster Grotto, (b) Shutterstock; p. 30: Shutterstock; p. 31: Images courtesy of Dreamworld@Gold Coast, Australia; p. 32: Images courtesy of Dreamworld@Gold Coast, Australia; p. 33: (t) Images courtesy of Dreamworld@Gold Coast, Australia, (b) Shutterstock; p. 34: Shutterstock; p. 35: AP Photo/HO; p. 36: AP Photo/Ho; p. 37: (t) Coasterimage.com, (b) Shutterstock; p. 38: Shutterstock; p. 39: Darren McCollester/Newsmakers; p. 40: AP Photo/The Repository, Joy Newcomb; p. 41: (t) AP Photo/The Republican, Christopher Evans; p. 42: Shutterstock; p. 43: Shutterstock; p. 44: (t) Celly-Mooney Photography/Corbis, (b) AP Photo/Lenox McLendon; p. 45: (t) Sam Morris/Las Vegas Sun/Reuters/Corbis, (b) Shutterstock; p. 46: (t) Howard Sayer/Alamy, (b) Hershey Entertainment & Resorts

Printed in the United States of America

1 2 3 4 5 6 7 8 9 14 13 12 11 10 09

TABLE OF CONTENTS

Words in the glossary appear in **bold** type
the first time they are used in the text.

THE ULTIMATE 10 Entertainment

AMUSEMENT PARK RIDES

Welcome to the Ultimate 10! This action-packed series puts you in the seat of some of the most amazing thrill rides in the world.

In this book, you will find out which rides are the biggest and best. You will hang on for every twist and turn. Each one will take you a bit closer to finding out what makes these exciting rides work.

Giant Drop in Australia is one of the ultimate thrill rides.

Amusement park rides can be one of the ultimate thrills. Where else can you feel the weightlessness of space? Where else can you feel the force of a fighter jet at takeoff? Where else can you be terrified and delighted at the same time?

Rides today are faster and taller than ever. This book will give you a behind-the-scenes look at 10 of the most memorable. Buckle up. Hang on. It is going to be one wild ride!

Scream Machines

Here are 10 amusement park rides that are guaranteed to thrill.

#**1** Kingda Ka

#**2** Millennium Force

#**3** Steel Dragon 2000

#**4** Son of Beast

#**5** Perilous Plunge

#**6** X^2

#**7** Giant Drop

#**8** Superman: The Escape

#**9** Superman: Ride of Steel

#**10** Stratosphere Tower

#1

KINGDA KA
Mean Green Scream Machine

When Kingda Ka opened on May 21, 2005, it shattered many roller coaster records. There is no ride as tall. There is no ride as fast. If you dare to ride Kingda Ka, you had better be brave. No other roller coaster can compare to this mean green scream machine.

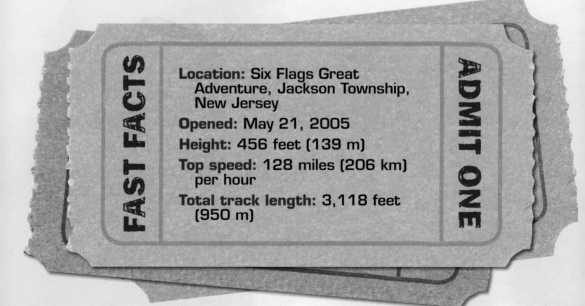

FAST FACTS

Location: Six Flags Great Adventure, Jackson Township, New Jersey

Opened: May 21, 2005

Height: 456 feet (139 m)

Top speed: 128 miles (206 km) per hour

Total track length: 3,118 feet (950 m)

ADMIT ONE

3-2-1, Blast Off!

To ride this massive coaster, you head to Six Flags Great Adventure in Jackson Township, New Jersey. You feel a bit nervous as you climb into the brightly colored train. Shoulder **restraints** lock you in place. Suddenly, you and 17 other riders are blasted down the track. It feels like a fighter jet taking off. You are rocketing along at a speed of 128 miles (206 kilometers) per hour in less than four seconds!

Before you can catch your breath, the train shoots you straight up toward the sky. There is nothing you can do now but scream! In seconds, you reach a peak that towers 456 feet (139 meters) high. That is taller than a 45-story building! The coaster is so tall that there are special lights on the track to keep airplanes from crashing into it.

Kingda Ka's thrills begin with a completely vertical climb.

"[Kingda Ka] goes so far above and beyond. This is like Xtreme sports, but five different ones combined into 40 seconds."

—Steven Urbanowicz, theme park and roller coaster historian

7

Twist and Turn

After a soaring turn, you race back down a twisting 418-foot (127-m) drop. That is the largest drop of any coaster in the world. It is just one more record that Kingda Ka holds. Your stomach churns as you whip through a spiral turn. You swoop down into a valley and then head toward a last hill that is 128 feet (39 m) tall. After all the twists, turns, and screaming, you glide gently into the unloading station. Your heart is still racing. Though it seemed like forever, the entire ride lasted less than one minute!

About 1,400 passengers can experience Kingda Ka's twisting drops each hour.

ROLLER COASTER RECORDS

TOP 10: TALLEST STEEL COASTERS

COASTER	LOCATION	HEIGHT
1. Kingda Ka	Six Flags Great Adventure (NJ)	456 feet (139 m)
2. Top Thrill Dragster	Cedar Point (OH)	420 feet (128 m)
3. Steel Dragon 2000	Nagashima Spa Land (Japan)	318 feet (97 m)
4. Millennium Force	Cedar Point (OH)	310 feet (94 m)
5. Thunder Dolphin	LaQua (Japan)	263 feet (80 m)
6. Fujiyama	Fuji-Q Highland (Japan)	259 feet (79 m)
7. Eejanaika	Fuji-Q Highland (Japan)	249 feet (76 m)
8. Titan	Six Flags Over Texas (TX)	245 feet (75 m)
9. Silver Star	Europa Park (Germany)	240 feet (73 m)
10. Goliath	Six Flags Magic Mountain (CA)	235 feet (72 m)

*Through 2008

A Thrill a Minute

Kingda Ka uses liquid to jumpstart its thrills. It relies on a **hydraulic** launch system. The coaster train is hooked to a giant cable. Thousands of gallons of fluid are pumped into huge motors that control the cable. Pressure and energy build up in the motors. To launch, that pressure is released. The cable whips the coaster train down the track at breakneck speed.

Riding Kingda Ka, you sometimes feel weightless. There are moments when you feel almost as much force as an astronaut taking off in the space shuttle. You might even think twice before riding on any coaster ever again. One thing is sure: You will never forget riding Kingda Ka.

Kingda Ka's tallest hill is three times taller than the Statue of Liberty.

DID YOU KNOW?

Most roller coasters have their own theme song or album. That is the music that blares through the speakers while riders load the train. Kingda Ka uses _Episode II_, an album by a Danish band called Safri Duo. The songs have a pulsing dance beat.

#2

MILLENNIUM FORCE

A Force to Be Reckoned With

The Millennium Force roller coaster met the year 2000 head-on. It was a new era. The day it opened in May 2000, Millennium Force broke a total of 12 roller coaster records. At the time, it was the fastest coaster in the world. Even today, few thrill rides can compare.

FAST FACTS

Location: Cedar Point, Sandusky, Ohio

Opened: May 13, 2000

Height: 310 feet (94 m)

Top speed: 92 miles (148 km) per hour

Total track length: 6,595 feet (2,010 m)

ADMIT ONE

Slow Climb to Terror

You can feel like an ant walking through Cedar Point amusement park in Sandusky, Ohio. A maze of massive steel thrill rides looms overhead. One of them is Millennium Force. Its huge blue steel hills soar above you as you wait in line to ride.

Once you are secure inside one of the blue, red, or yellow trains, it is go time. You are slowly pulled up the first hill. It is 310 feet (94 m) tall! All you can see in front of you is steel and sky. You reach the top, and your heart pounds as you plummet almost straight down for 300 feet (91 m). By now, you are rocketing along at 92 miles (148 km) per hour.

"I loved it! That first drop, you get lifted right out of your seat."

—coaster expert Jim Raimar

A train of 36 terrified passengers is about to zoom down Millennium Force's giant first hill.

Fantastic Force

Millennium Force is not yet through with you. You whip into a hard right turn as you climb 169 feet (52 m). Then, you pass through a tunnel before zipping over a 182-foot (55-m) hill that leaves you weightless. Next, you roar through three more turns, through another tunnel, over a small hill, and up through a hard right turn. After 2 minutes and 20 seconds, you coast to a stop. Wow!

> **"Millennium Force [introduces] the world to a whole new level of roller coaster riding."**
> —Don Miears, former general manager of Cedar Point amusement park

Millennium Force includes a 300-foot (91-m) drop.

QUICK HITS

THRILL RIDE CITY

Cedar Point amusement park in Sandusky, Ohio, holds the record for most coasters in a single park. It has a total of 17. In addition to Millennium Force, there are other heart-stopping rides in the park. At one time, Top Thrill Dragster (right) was the tallest steel coaster in the world. The park also boasts Mean Streak, one of the seventh-fastest wooden coasters in the world.

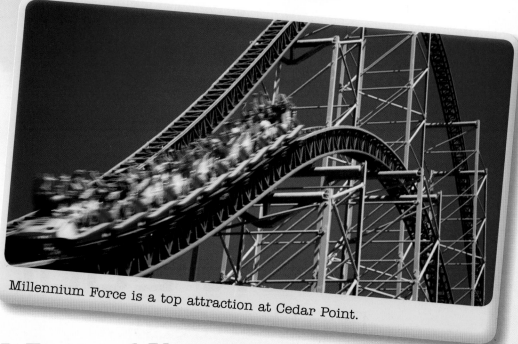

Millennium Force is a top attraction at Cedar Point.

A Force of Nature

Like all coasters, Millennium Force uses the force of **gravity** to deliver its thrills and chills. A motor uses a cable to pull the train up the first hill. After the train reaches the top, gravity takes over. What goes up must come down.

Gravity pulls the train down the hill. No other machine is needed to power the coaster. The train gains so much speed that it can easily climb the rest of the hills. This buildup of speed is called **momentum**. It is enough to keep a coaster going until the very last scream.

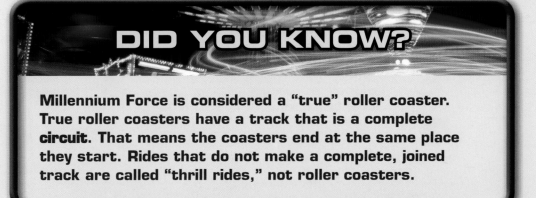

DID YOU KNOW?

Millennium Force is considered a "true" roller coaster. True roller coasters have a track that is a complete **circuit**. That means the coasters end at the same place they start. Rides that do not make a complete, joined track are called "thrill rides," not roller coasters.

#3

STEEL DRAGON 2000
Far East Fear

Extreme thrill rides may be taking over the world. Americans are not the only people who love to ride these scary steel monsters. Japan is home to some of the most fast, furious, and frightening thrill rides in the world. One of the biggest is Steel Dragon 2000.

FAST FACTS

Location: Nagashima Spa Land, Mie, Japan

Opened: August 1, 2000

Height: 310 feet (94 m)

Top speed: 93 miles (150 km) per hour

Total track length: 8,133 feet (2,479 m)

ADMIT ONE

The Year of the Dragon

Steel Dragon 2000 opened a few months after Millennium Force. When it opened, it beat many of Millennium Force's world records. Many of its records have been broken too, but Steel Dragon 2000 is still the longest steel coaster in the world. It is 8,133 feet (2,479 m) of stone-cold steel terror.

Steel Dragon 2000 may not impress you with its looks. It is not a flashy color, like some other rides. Your jaw will drop at its size, however. It is huge! The chains slowly pull your train up the first hill. Seconds tick by as you face the sky, wondering what will come next.

> "It takes every coaster thrill you've ever had and magnifies it by about a thousand."
>
> —Scott Rutherford, author of *The American Roller Coaster*

Steel Dragon is the tallest coaster outside of the United States.

Hang Tight for a Long Ride

There is nothing slow about what happens next. You rocket down a 318-foot (97-m) hill at blazing speed. You are immediately whipped up a 252-foot (77-m) hill. You get **airtime** for just a second before the train races back down. You can barely hang on as you are blasted through two giant, curved turns. As the ride nears the end, you glide over smaller hills and through two tunnels. That long ride lasted a heart-pounding three minutes.

> Steel Dragon 2000 features two huge drops.

ROLLER COASTER RECORDS

LONGEST STEEL COASTERS

Japan boasts some of the biggest and best rides outside the United States. The country has three of the longest steel coasters in the world.

COASTER	LOCATION	TOTAL TRACK LENGTH
1. Steel Dragon 2000	Nagashima Spa Land (Japan)	8,133 feet (2,479 m)
2. Daidarasaurus	Expoland (Japan)	7,677 feet (2,340 m)
3. Ultimate	Lightwater Valley (UK)	7,442 feet (2,268 m)
4. Fujiyama	Fuji-Q Highland (Japan)	6,708 feet (2,045 m)
5. Millennium Force	Cedar Point (OH)	6,595 feet (2,010 m)

*Through 2008

Shaking Things Up

Japan is a country that has many earthquakes. An earthquake can topple a building. It can destroy a bridge. Japanese **engineers** always have to consider how large structures will survive earthquakes. They have to be able to take the shaking without falling apart.

So how can a giant roller coaster be built to survive a quake? The builders of Steel Dragon 2000 used extra steel for support. Much of this steel was used to make superstrong support columns. This made Steel Dragon 2000 expensive to build. It cost more than $50 million! It is one of the most expensive roller coasters in the world.

A massive earthquake hit Japan in 1995. Ride designers must make sure that their rides can survive a quake.

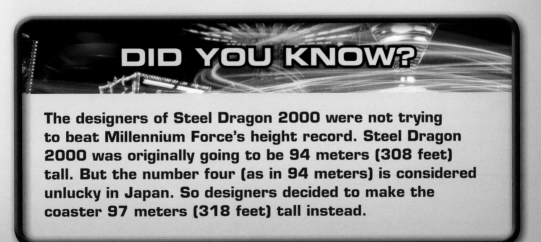

DID YOU KNOW?

The designers of Steel Dragon 2000 were not trying to beat Millennium Force's height record. Steel Dragon 2000 was originally going to be 94 meters (308 feet) tall. But the number four (as in 94 meters) is considered unlucky in Japan. So designers decided to make the coaster 97 meters (318 feet) tall instead.

#4

SON OF BEAST
Wicked, Wooden, and Wild

Wooden roller coasters are not as sleek as steel coasters. They do not usually reach the massive size or speeds of their steel cousins. That changed when Son of Beast came along in May 2000. It shattered many records for wooden coasters. It was the tallest and the fastest. It was also the first wooden coaster with a loop.

FAST FACTS

Location: Kings Island, Cincinnati, Ohio

Opened: May 26, 2000

Height: 218 feet (66 m)

Top speed: 78 miles (126 km) per hour

Total track length: 7,032 feet (2,143 m)

ADMIT ONE

Runaway Train

Son of Beast toys with you at first. The first hill is only a 51-foot (16-m) drop. The wooden boards grumble and growl as you pick up speed. Wooden coasters are supposed to be bumpy. That's one thing that sets them apart from steel coasters—and makes them so much fun.

You hold on for dear life as you are whipped through turns. Then, you start to climb the huge, 218-foot (66-m) hill of wood. You are sent roaring straight back down.

"The roughest ride I had ever ridden, it even gave me two bruises."
—*Coaster Grotto* review

More than 300 miles (almost 500 km) of wood was used to make Son of Beast.

Shake, Rattle, and Roll

It feels as if the ride will shake apart as you head into spirals. Not just one spiral, but two! The wooden track rumbles like a wild animal as you make one final swooping turn and drop. Then, you ease back into the station, your bones still shaking.

Baseball star Ken Griffey Jr. and his son Trey get ready to ride Son of Beast. About 1,000 people ride the coaster every hour.

ROLLER COASTER RECORDS

TOP 10: TALLEST WOODEN COASTERS

COASTER	LOCATION	HEIGHT
1. Son of Beast	Kings Island (OH)	218 feet (66 m)
2. Colossos	Heide Park (Germany)	196 feet (60 m)
3. T Express	Everland (South Korea)	184 feet (56 m)
4. El Toro	Six Flags Great Adventure (NJ)	181 feet (55 m)
5. Rattler	Six Flags Fiesta Texas (TX)	179 feet (55 m)
6. The Voyage	Holiday World (IN)	163 feet (50 m)
7. Mean Streak	Cedar Point (OH)	161 feet (49 m)
8. Texas Giant	Six Flags Over Texas (TX)	143 feet (44 m)
9. White Cyclone	Nagashima Spa Land (Japan)	139 feet (42 m)
10. Hades	Mt. Olympus Park (WI)	136 feet (41 m)

*Through 2008

Out of the Loop

Son of Beast is made of thick pieces of wood. The loop was one of the hardest parts to build. Thick wood cannot be bent into a curve, so the loop has a steel frame that is covered with wood.

Son of Beast's huge loop proved to be a problem. So did its heavy trains. Both put a strain on the wooden track, causing it to weaken and crack. In 2006, 27 people were hurt in an accident. The roller coaster was closed. Park officials decided to remove the record-breaking loop to make the ride safer. They also added lighter trains. Today, Son of Beast runs without the loop.

Workers inspect Son of Beast's curved wooden tracks. The safety of the riders is a top concern of every thrill ride designer.

DID YOU KNOW?

Son of Beast is not the only huge wooden roller coaster at Kings Island. Its concept was based on another coaster in the park called the Beast. While Son of Beast may be taller and faster, it is not longer. The Beast holds the record for longest wooden coaster. It is a bone-rattling 7,359 feet (2,243 m) long!

#5

PERILOUS PLUNGE
Super Soaker

What happens when you cross a roller coaster with raging rapids? You get Perilous Plunge. It is the tallest and steepest water ride in the world. Riders rush down a 115-foot (35-m) hill toward a huge splash. If you want to ride Perilous Plunge, you'd better be ready to get wet.

FAST FACTS

Location: Knott's Berry Farm, Buena Park, California

Opened: September 2000

Height: 121 feet (37 m)

Top speed: 50 miles (80 km) per hour

Total track length: 865 feet (264 m)

ADMIT ONE

Scream and Splash

The first thing you notice is how huge the boats on Perilous Plunge are. Each one weighs 7 tons (6 metric tons). That's as much as an average school bus! You climb inside with 23 other passengers and look out at the calm water. It looks harmless enough. How bad could it be? Before you have time to relax, you start the slow climb upward. Each click of the lift chain takes you closer -to the sky.

At the top, you are 121 feet (37 m) above the ground. That is just 34 feet (10 m) less than the height of Niagara Falls! Then, you take the plunge. You are whipped back in your seat as you plummet almost straight down. It feels like jumping off a waterfall.

"Water begins hitting you in the face and body and pours into the boat."
—newspaper reporter Danielle Herbin

The steepest hill in Perilous Plunge is at a 78-degree angle.

A CLASSIC THRILL

Water rides are called **flumes.** Flumes have gotten taller and scarier over the years. They are not a new idea, however. Shoot-the-chute rides have been around since the late 1800s. Back then, large flat boats were pulled up a ramp by poles, chains, or ropes. The boats then slid down the tall ramp. At the bottom was a large pool of water or even a river. The flat-bottomed boat skidded and skipped across the water with a bumpy splash.

Super Soaker

All you can do is scream. A spray of water stings your face as you head toward the lagoon below. As you hit bottom, you are drenched with water. You are not the only one. The giant boat splashes a wall of water 45 feet (14 m) high. Anyone walking near the ride gets soaking wet, too!

About 1,900 riders get soaked on Perilous Plunge each hour.

Water, Water Everywhere

Perilous Plunge uses a basic chain-lift system to pull the boat to the top of the hill. Once at the top, the boat hits water. It takes a lot of water to run Perilous Plunge. There are 40,000 gallons (150,000 liters) of water pumped to the top each minute.

Like many coasters, Perilous Plunge uses magnet brakes to help provide a smooth stop. **Electrical currents** cause magnets to **attract** the brakes to the metal rails. This process slows the boat as it falls. Perilous Plunge was the first flume ride to use underwater magnet brakes.

Perilous Plunge begins with one big hill.

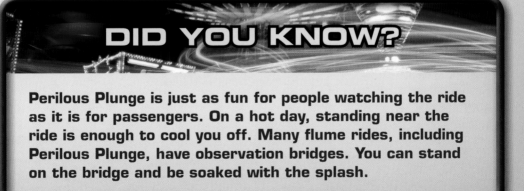

DID YOU KNOW?

Perilous Plunge is just as fun for people watching the ride as it is for passengers. On a hot day, standing near the ride is enough to cool you off. Many flume rides, including Perilous Plunge, have observation bridges. You can stand on the bridge and be soaked with the splash.

#6

X²
A New Dimension in Thrills

Whipping through turns and loops on a roller coaster can be scary.
On most roller coasters, though, you have the train floor beneath
your feet and the train car around you for comfort. Not on X²!
Riding this coaster, the only thing between you and the ground
is air. This ride is not for the faint of heart.

FAST FACTS

Location: Six Flags Magic
    Mountain, Valencia, California
Opened: January 12, 2002
Height: 175 feet (53 m)
Top speed: 76 miles (122 km)
    per hour
Total track length: 3,610 feet
    (1,100 m)

ADMIT ONE

When you ride X², your legs dangle in the air. This adds to the feeling that you're hurtling out of control through the sky.

Hanging In There

X² is the world's first "fourth dimension" coaster. Most roller coasters operate in three dimensions. They move forward and backward. They move up and down. They move left and right. On this new type of ride, a move is added, and that new move is you! Your seat spins as the train flies along the track. It is an incredibly out-of-control feeling.

Before the ride starts, large, colorful shoulder harnesses lock you in place in your seat. There is no escape. The train climbs to the top of a giant hill. Then, you are blasted down a 215-foot (66-m) drop facedown. Your feet hang free you as your seat turns wildly.

X² is a series of extreme drops, twists, and turns.

Pushed to the Extreme

You don't know which way you will turn next. You can't tell where you are. Up is down. Left is right. As the coaster gains speed, you spin completely around. It all happens at blazing-fast speed. You race through flips and turns along 3,610 feet (1,100 m) of twisted steel.

> **"X²** grabs you ... and squeezes you until your heart pops out of your throat."
> —Brian MacDonald,
> *Los Angeles Times*

QUICK HITS

A FEW OF THE FOURTH

Fourth dimension roller coasters are a new invention. There are only four of them in the world!

COASTER	LOCATION	YEAR OPENED
X²	Six Flags Magic Mountain (CA)	2002
Eejanaika	Fuji-Q Highland (Japan)	2006
Kirnu	Linnanmäki (Finland)	2007
Inferno	Terra Mitica (Spain)	2007

*Through 2008

Sit and Scream

The train and seats on X^2 are like those of no other roller coaster in the United States. The first difference is size. The train is huge! It is 20 feet (6 m) wide and 70 feet (21 m) long. It is as wide as three regular roller coaster trains. The seats are like wings connected to the outside of the train.

Gears inside the train move the seats. Two seat-rotation rails along the track move the gears. The rotation rails bend up and down slightly. As the train races over the rails, the bends hit the gears and move them. This spins the seats as the train speeds down the track.

A train on X^2 moves up the first hill. Because riders sit backward, they don't know exactly when they'll start their first terrifying drop.

DID YOU KNOW?

Speakers by your head blare out music while you ride X^2. The music has to be pretty loud to be heard above all the screaming. The playlist includes five songs: "It Had to Be You" by Harry Connick Jr., "Enter Sandman" by Metallica, "Love in an Elevator" by Aerosmith, "Sabotage" by the Beastie Boys, and "Wake Up" by Rage Against the Machine. X^2 also has special effects like fog and flamethrowers along the track.

GIANT DROP
Falling for Fun

Dreamworld is the largest amusement park in Australia. But don't let the name fool you. Not all the dreams at this amusement park are nice. Giant Drop is a nightmare thrill ride. It is the closest you may ever get to a skydiving free fall.

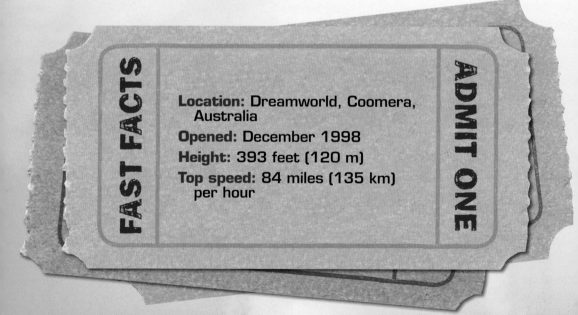

FAST FACTS

Location: Dreamworld, Coomera, Australia
Opened: December 1998
Height: 393 feet (120 m)
Top speed: 84 miles (135 km) per hour

ADMIT ONE

Towering Thrills

A drop tower is one of the ultimate thrill rides. It takes your fear of falling to new extremes. Giant Drop is the tallest drop tower in the world. It reaches a dizzying 393 feet (120 m) into the sky.

From the ground, you have to bend your neck all the way back as you strain to see the top of the tower. You start to get nervous as you are secured into the seat. Your feet dangle just above the concrete. Then, you feel yourself slowly pulled skyward. Each second takes you farther and farther from the safe ground below.

The GIANT Drop
DREAMWORLD GOLD COAST AUSTRALIA

> **"I loved it! There is nothing like it. It doesn't matter how many times I ride, it always makes me scream!"**
> —Giant Drop rider

Hold on! Riding Giant Drop, you climb to the height of a 39-story building.

As you fall on Giant Drop, you are actually lifted a little out of your seat. Good thing you're wearing a safety harness!

Ultimate Airtime

The people and trees below you look like little specks. Then, you reach the top. You have one terrifying moment to look around before you drop. Your hair stands on end as you fall straight down at 84 miles (135 km) per hour. It takes only six terrifying seconds to reach the ground.

RECORD BREAKERS

TALLEST TOWERS
Eight drop towers reach 300 feet (91 m) or higher:

DROP TOWER	LOCATION	HEIGHT
1. Giant Drop	Dreamworld (Australia)	393 feet (120 m)
2. Blue Fall	Yokohama (Japan)	351 feet (107 m)
3. Drop Zone Stunt Tower	Kings Island (OH)	315 feet (96 m)
4. Superman: Tower of Power	Six Flags Over Texas (TX)	313 feet (95 m)
5. Supreme Scream	Knott's Berry Farm (CA)	312 feet (95 m)
6. Riddler's Revenge	WB Movie World (Spain)	310 feet (94 m)
7. Drop Zone Stunt Tower	Kings Dominion (VA)	305 feet (93 m)
8. Power Tower	Cedar Point (OH)	300 feet (91 m)

*Through 2008

There is also a Giant Drop in the United States. It is located at Six Flags Great America in Chicago, Illinois. It is much smaller than its Australian cousin. This Great Drop is only 227 feet (69 m) tall.

Double the Terror

Dreamworld's Giant Drop shares its tower with another thrill ride, Tower of Terror. Giant Drop riders are hauled to the top and dropped on the east and west sides of the tower. Tower of Terror riders are shot straight up an L-shaped track on another side of the tower. They blast upward to 377 feet (115 m). Their train reaches a blazing 100 miles (160 km) per hour. Then, the train free-falls back down the track.

It took 450 tons (408 metric tons) of steel to build the tower that supports the two rides. The Tower of Terror ride shakes the massive tower. This adds even more thrills to the riders high on the Giant Drop ride.

The Tower of Terror train climbs 38 stories high.

SUPERMAN: THE ESCAPE
Superhero Scare

Look! Up in the sky! It's a bird! It's a plane! No, it's Superman: The Escape. This insane thrill ride is a shuttle coaster. Unlike a true roller coaster, it does not make a full circuit. It is shaped more like an out-of-control L. And is it fast! It was the first thrill ride in the world to top 100 miles (160 km) per hour.

FAST FACTS

Location: Six Flags Magic Mountain, Valencia, California

Opened: March 15, 1997

Height: 415 feet (126 m)

Top speed: 100 miles (160 km) per hour

Total track length: 1,235 feet (376 m)

ADMIT ONE

Faster Than a Speeding Bullet

Superman: The Escape is full of thrills and chills before you even board the train. Standing in line for the ride, you come to the Fortress of Solitude. It looks like an enormous, icy cave. Pulsing lights, glowing paint, and loud music surround you. There is no telling what may be waiting for you through the doors at the end of the cave.

The doors swing open and you board the train. You are pinned against your seat as the train takes off like a shot. It takes only seven seconds for the train to reach its top speed of 100 miles (160 km) per hour. Just when you thought it could not get scarier, you head upward.

> "This is far different than any ride in the history of the outdoor amusement industry."
>
> —Paul Rubens, editor of *Park World* magazine

Riders on Superman: The Escape shoot straight up and then come straight back down.

Superman: The Escape can handle 1,050 riders per hour.

More Powerful Than a Locomotive

You are shot straight up a tower 415 feet (126 m) tall. You barely have time to catch your breath before you start falling backward. That's when the real screaming begins. You are completely weightless for a few moments. Then, the speed picks back up before you roar into the station. The entire terrifying ride lasts a little more than 20 seconds!

QUICK HITS

THE KINGS OF COASTERS

Does Superman: The Escape look a lot like the Tower of Terror in Australia? That's because they were both designed by the same company: Intamin AG. The Swiss company has designed many of the most amazing thrill rides today. The designers at Intamin AG created Millennium Force and Kingda Ka. They also designed Tower of Terror and Top Thrill Dragster. The thrill-ride experts at Intamin are always trying to push the limits of speed and height.

You feel **4.5** times the force of gravity when Superman: The Escape takes off. That is more force than an astronaut feels taking off in a space shuttle.

Heroic Adventure

It is not just speed and height that make Superman: The Escape an amazing ride. It also has a powerful launch system. The entire system is powered by magnets.

Strong electrical currents react with high-powered magnets. There are magnets on the bottom of the train and on the track. The electrical currents change how the magnets react to one another. The magnets **repel** each other, to slingshot the coaster train down the track at blazing-fast speeds. The same magnets also attract each other, to slow the train and stop it.

The trains in Superman: The Escape hurtle down the track because of the power of magnets.

#9

SUPERMAN: RIDE OF STEEL
Superman Strikes Again

Not all Superman rides are created equal. One of them stands out from the rest. That ride is Superman: Ride of Steel, at Six Flags New England. Coaster experts have voted it the best steel coaster on the planet. The Ride of Steel proves that a coaster does not have to be the fastest or the tallest to be the best.

FAST FACTS

Location: Six Flags New England, Springfield, Massachusetts

Opened: May 13, 2000

Height: 208 feet (63 m)

Top speed: 77 miles (124 km) per hour

Total track length: 5,400 feet (1,646 m)

ADMIT ONE

Nonstop Super Thrills

Superman: Ride of Steel has all the elements needed for an excellent roller coaster ride. It has amazing drops, twisting turns, tunnels, and the speed to back it all up. What makes this ride so great is the nonstop action. The pace never slows down. You experience one thrill after another on this ride.

You brace yourself as the train climbs to the top of the lift hill. Then, you rocket down a 221-foot (67-m) drop and straight toward one of two underground tunnels. You plunge into the darkness. You are blasting down the track at 77 miles (124 km) per hour.

> **"Its massive drops, intense airtime and an awesome twisted second half make it one epic ride."**
> —David Fraser, roller coaster reviewer

Superman: Ride of Steel thrills fans with its nonstop action.

QUICK HITS

SUPERMAN VERSUS MILLENNIUM FORCE

Each year, the newspaper *Amusement Today* ranks the best coasters in the country. The winner earns the Golden Ticket Award. It is the ultimate award for coasters. Superman: Ride of Steel battled it out with Millennium Force for the number one spot for seven years.

	Superman: Ride of Steel	Millennium Force
2001	2	1
2002	2	1
2003	1	2
2004	2	1
2005	2	1
2006	1	2
2007	1	2
2008	1	2

More Powerful Than Kryptonite

In seconds, you are launched out of the tunnel and up a second hill. You hold on tight as you race around a tight turn. You are sent screaming over two more hills. Your stomach churns. Then, you spin through not one twisting spiral **helix**, but two. There is no time to catch your breath as you plunge into another pitch-black tunnel. You hit one final bone-rattling turn as you head back to the train station.

On Superman: Ride of Steel, thrill seekers head through twists and turns while upside down.

Super Safety

Since opening in 2000, Superman: Ride of Steel has been improved to make it safer. The ride received additional brakes. Seat belts and T-bar restraints were strengthened and improved. A special computer system was also added. The ride will not launch until the computer senses that every restraint is safely in place.

Safety is not the only thing changing on Superman: Ride of Steel. Plans are in the works to add special effects. There will be fog and fire bursts. Riders will also enjoy a thumping new onboard sound system.

Safety restraints are vital on a ride like Superman: Ride of Steel.

DID YOU KNOW?

There are several versions of Superman: Ride of Steel. There is a Superman: Ride of Steel in Darien Lake, New York. One is in Upper Marlboro, Maryland. Another is near Washington, D.C. There's even one near Madrid, Spain! There are also other Superman-themed coasters. There are a couple of coasters named Superman: Ultimate Flight. There are three Superman: Tower of Power rides, too!

#10
STRATOSPHERE TOWER
Reaching New Heights

Some of the most extreme thrill rides are not found in an amusement park. Instead, they sit atop a tower 1,149 feet (350 m) tall in Las Vegas, Nevada. The Stratosphere Tower supports three ultimate thrill rides: Big Shot, X-Scream, and Insanity: The Ride. Riding them is one of the ultimate thrill-ride experiences.

FAST FACTS

Location: Stratosphere Tower and Hotel, Las Vegas, Nevada

Tower height: 1,149 feet (350 m)

Big Shot height: 1,081 feet (329 m)

Insanity height: more than 900 feet (275 m)

X-Scream height: 866 feet (264 m)

ADMIT ONE

The 16 riders on Big Shot shoot up 160 feet (49 m) in 2 seconds. Then they free-fall above Las Vegas.

On Top of the World

The rides on the Stratosphere Tower would not be anything special on the ground. It is their extreme height that makes them so terrifying. The first ride you visit is Big Shot. You board the ride on a platform a dizzying 921 feet (281 m) above the streets of Las Vegas. Your shoulder harness is fastened in place. You hold on for dear life as you are blasted straight up at 45 miles (72 km) per hour. At the top, you are 1,081 feet (329 m) in the air! Then, you free-fall back down to the tower deck before bounding back up again.

"[Big Shot] is beyond frightening— this is the scariest ride I know."

—Scott Rutherford, author of *The American Roller Coaster*

X-Scream shoots riders out over the edge of the Stratosphere Tower. Riders feel as if they might fall 900 feet (275 m) to the ground below.

Over the Edge

Next, you climb aboard X-Scream, the world's scariest teeter-totter. The shoulder harness locks in place. Then, the track lifts you up. The ride seems harmless enough until it starts to tilt. As it tilts, your car plummets down over the edge of the tower. You are left screaming and hanging in midair until the ride snaps you back to the safety of the tower. Then, you plunge over and back again and again.

QUICK HITS

THE HIGH ROLLER

In 1996, a roller coaster opened on top of the Stratosphere Tower. The High Roller wasn't particularly fast. It didn't have any loops or extreme hills. But it was the highest coaster in the world, which gave it a thrill all its own. The High Roller was removed from the tower in 2005.

Defying Gravity

The wildest ride on the Stratosphere Tower is Insanity: The Ride. You climb on what looks like a demented octopus. A giant steel arm swings you around until you are dangling more than 900 feet (275 m) above the ground. Then, the ride starts to spin. As it spins faster, you are pulled outward. You scream as you are looking straight down at the streets of Las Vegas.

Insanity: the Ride uses **centrifugal force**. When something spins very fast, it is pulled outward. The faster Insanity spins, the more the seats are pulled outward. Eventually, they are nearly straight out, facing the streets far below. Unless you close your eyes, you have no choice but to look straight down as you spin.

Thrill seekers on Insanity: The Ride spin around at 40 miles (64 km) per hour.

DID YOU KNOW?

There have been a few terrifying moments on Insanity and X-Scream that were not part of the fun. Twice, the rides broke down. One time was due to a power outage. The other was due to high winds. Horrified riders were left hanging in the air until workers could rescue them.

Colossus

Thorpe Park, Chertsey, England

Colossus may not be the tallest or the fastest ride. What it does have is stomach-turning **inversions**. Inversions are loops, spirals, and turns during which a rider is turned upside down. Most coasters have one or two at the most. Colossus has a total of 10!

Colossus reaches a speed of 45 miles (72 km) per hour. Riders twist and turn through 2,789 feet (850 m) of steel. An exact copy of the ride was built in China.

Fahrenheit

Hersheypark, Hershey, Pennsylvania

Fahrenheit opened in 2008. Its slogan is "97 degrees and falling fast." This new coaster goes way beyond vertical. It has one of the few drops in the world that are more than 90 degrees. After a 121-foot (37-m) climb to the top of the first hill, the train does not merely head straight down. It actually curves backward!

The 97-degree drop is one of the steepest drops of any coaster in the United States. It is so steep that you cannot see the track below you as you plummet downward. To add to the thrill, riders are whipped through six different inversions.

Glossary

airtime: the feeling of leaving your seat and hanging in the air

attract: to cause things to pull toward each other

centrifugal force: the force that causes an object to be pulled outward from the center by spinning

circuit: a complete track in which a ride's end and beginning meet

electrical currents: the flow of electricity

engineers: people who are trained to plan and design the building of an amusement park ride

flumes: narrow chutes full of flowing water

gravity: the force that pulls objects downward

helix: a spiral curved turn

hydraulic: powered by the use of pressurized liquid

inversions: loops or turns during which a rider is turned upside down

momentum: the force or speed of movement

repel: to cause things to push away from each other

restraints: a system of belts or bars designed to keep ride passengers safe in their seats

For More Information

Books

Lepora, Nathan. *High-Speed Thrills* (The Science Behind Thrill Rides). Pleasantville, NY: Gareth Stevens, 2008.

Mason, Paul. *Roller Coaster!* (Motion and Acceleration). Chicago: Raintree, 2006.

Mitchell, Susan K. *The Biggest Thrill Rides* (Megastructures). Pleasantville, NY: Gareth Stevens Publishing, 2008.

Stone, Lynn M. *Roller Coasters.* Vero Beach, FL: Rourke Publishing, 2002.

Web Sites

Discovery Kids: Build Your Own Coaster
http://kids.discovery.com/games/ rollercoasters/buildacoaster.html
See what kind of thrill ride you can build!

Learner: Design a Roller Coaster
www.learner.org/exhibits/parkphysics/coaster
See what it takes to design a great ride.

Ultimate Roller Coaster
www.ultimaterollercoaster.com
Read reviews of the best roller coasters.

Publisher's note to educators and parents: Our editors have carefully reviewed these web sites to ensure that they are suitable for children. Many web sites change frequently, however, and we cannot guarantee that a site's future contents will continue to meet our high standards of quality and educational value. Be advised that children should be closely supervised whenever they access the Internet.

Index

About the Author

Susan K. Mitchell is a huge fan of amusement park rides! She is a teacher and the author of several picture books. Susan has also written more than 20 nonfiction chapter books for young readers. She lives near Houston, Texas, with her husband and daughters. Susan dedicates this book to Emily and Rachel, who make life full of thrills.